What Does A Police Dog Do?

Ellen F. Feld

Photographed by John Cebula

*Dedicated to all the K-9s,
who work hard every day, with a wag in their tail, to keep their communities safe.*

This book would not be possible without the assistance of many people and organizations. First, thanks to Trooper Patrick Clayton, who was instrumental in getting this project started and connecting the author with many K-9s and their handlers. I'd also like to thank the Massachusetts State Police Fire and Explosion Investigation Section, assigned to the Massachusetts State Fire Marshal's office, the Holyoke Fire Department in Holyoke, MA, as well as the Easthampton, MA Police Department, the Amherst, MA Police Department and the Russell, MA Police Department.

Copyright © 2022 by Ellen F. Feld
Published by Willow Bend Publishing

All rights reserved, including the right of reproduction in part or in whole in any form.

Library of Congress Catalog Card Number: 2022906495

ISBN: 978-1-7337674-6-0

Direct inquiries to: Willow Bend Publishing
P.O. Box 304
Goshen, MA 01032
www.willowbendpublishing.com

Photography by John Cebula
Book design by Creative Publishing Book Design

Printed in USA

Meet Bijou (pronounced Bee-zhoo)!
She is a police dog.

Police dogs do many different things from fire investigations...

to searching for people.

Sometimes police dogs wear special outfits to protect them or let people know they are working.

Some police dogs help their human partners find out if a fire was started on purpose (that's called arson). They are trained to smell just one drop of accelerant, which is a substance that makes a fire burn faster. The dogs need to be able to identify many different liquids that are used as accelerants.

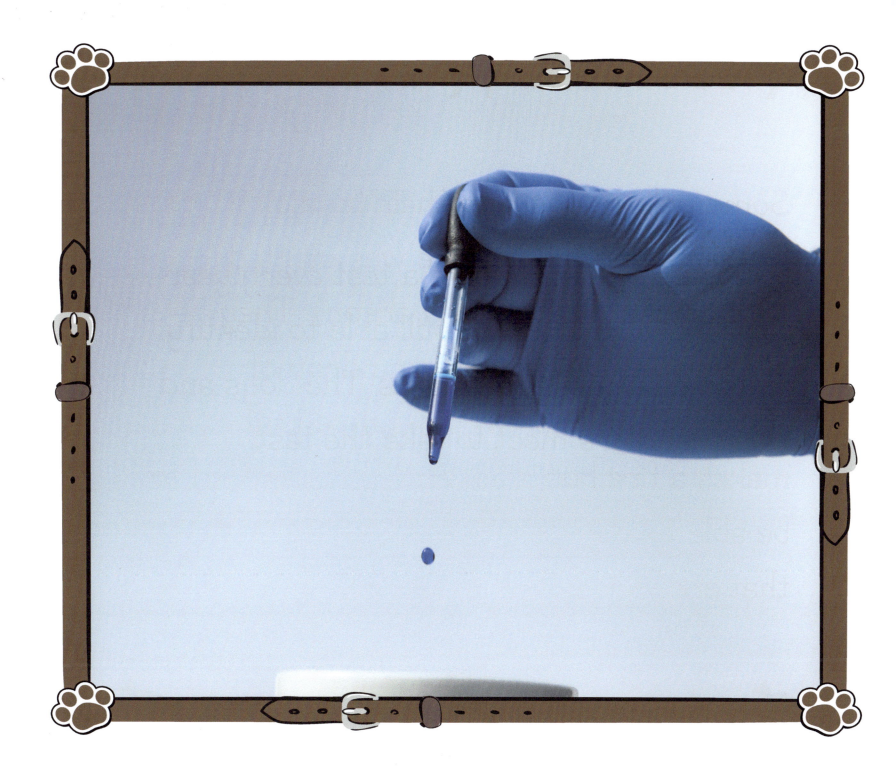

Arson dogs have to take a test every year to make sure they are still able to identify all the different accelerants. The dogs and their handlers meet to take the test.

For the test, four tin cans are nailed to a wooden wheel. One drop of accelerant is placed into one can and then all the cans are filled with burnt papers, clothes or other things that might be found at a fire.

Curtis smells each can and when he finds the one that has the accelerant, he sits down to signal to his handler that he found it. The reward for finding the accelerant is a piece of kibble (dog food). Many departments use Labrador retrievers as arson dogs because they will do just about anything for a little snack!

Bijou is asked by her handler to check another can, but she has already found the accelerant, so she sits and signals.

After he passes his test, Zach celebrates with his handler.

Bijou has been called to a fire! Was the fire set on purpose?

Bijou is asked to search the building and find the accelerant.

She found it!

Bomb dogs are trained to sniff out explosives. Many times they have to go to crowded places like sports events so dog breeds that like to be around people, like Labrador retrievers, are a popular choice for this work.

Bomb dogs have to check every part of every vehicle that comes into an event.

When not searching cars, Witten likes to watch the other dogs work, while Link absolutely loves to jump in place, over and over. Silly dog!

Winston is a comfort dog. He is very gentle and loves getting hugs. If someone has been hurt or in an accident, he may be called to come in and help that person feel better.

Winston will even go to a school to help the students have fun while they study for final exams.

Gino is a Belgian Malinois and is trained to search for people. He has found hikers lost in the woods...

and can even find a small metal object like a flashlight that has been hidden in a field. He doesn't smell the metal but can find the human scent on the metal.

When he finds the object, Gino will signal to his handler by lying down.

His reward is his favorite chew toy.

The Belgian Malinois is a popular choice for high energy jobs like building searches. If someone is hiding anywhere in a building, Gino may be asked to go into the building and find that person.

Gino will look everywhere and when he finds the scent of the person he is searching for...

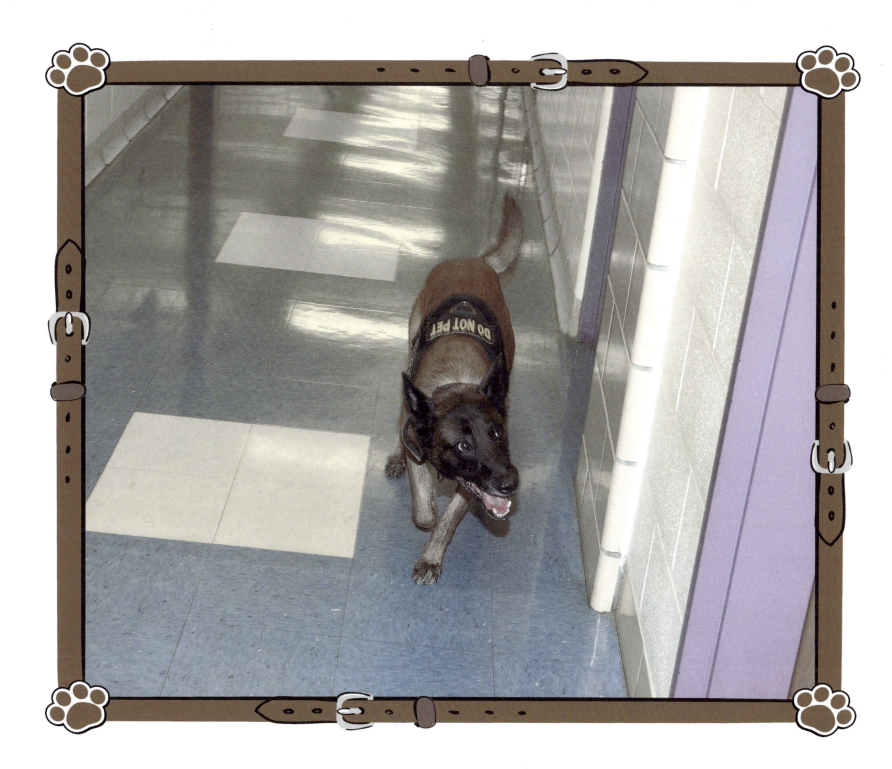

he will signal to his handler...

and get his favorite chew toy as a reward.

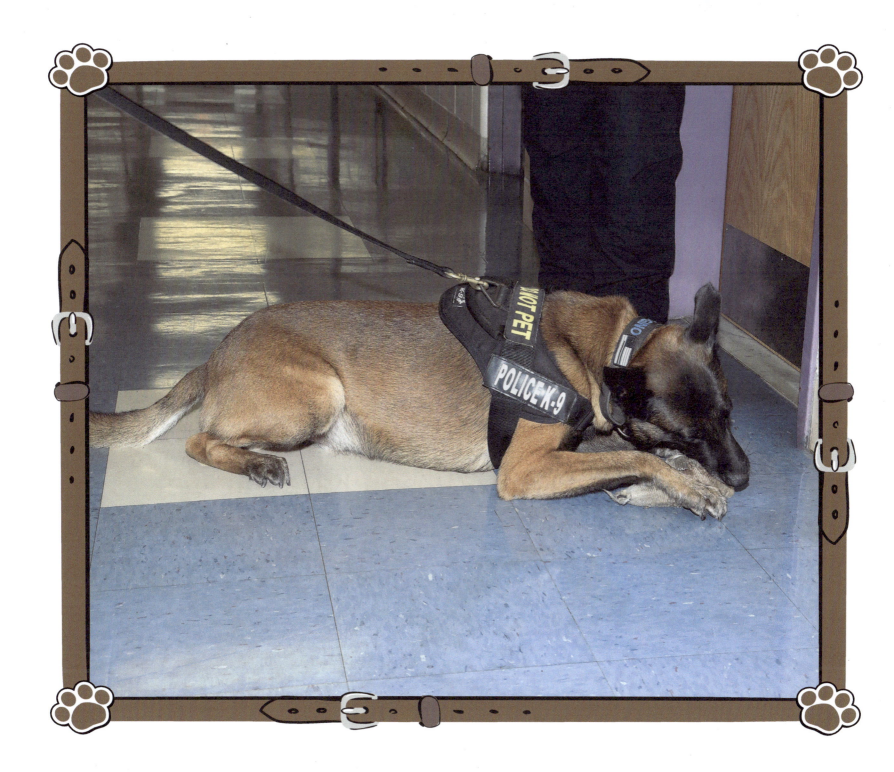

Police dogs are very important in aiding law enforcement and are loved and cared for by their handlers. So at the end of the work day, these dogs go home with their handlers and get to play and have fun, just like other dogs.

Bijou at the ocean.

Visit Willow Bend Publishing to Discover Other Best-Selling Animal Books

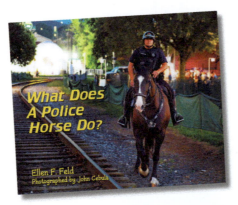
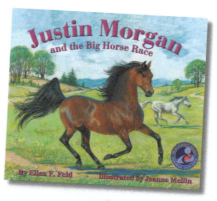
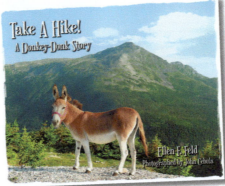

www.willowbendpublishing.com